RU In Control?

Written by Aimée Jackson

Contents

Social media
R U in control of it?

Chapter 1

to social media

Page 6

Chapter 2

to social media

Page 10

Fake news
R U in control of it?

Chapter 3
Talking about the news
Page 18

Chapter 4
Reading about the news
Page 24

Chapter 5
Hearing about the news
Page 28

Chapter 6
So, let's take control over what we read and hear!
Page 31

Chapter 7
Sharing the news
Page 35

Chapter 8
So, let's take control over fake news!
Page 39

Chapter 9
I can spot fake news! I am in control!
Page 43

Chapter 10
Advice
Page 47

Social media
R U in control of it?

Social media. It's everywhere. You may use it and you definitely know someone who does. Friends and family — everyone is on social media these days.

But are you in control of it?

You may be thinking yes, after all it is your social media and you control what you do on it. So yes you are in control of YOUR social media.

But are you in control of what you see on social media? Is anyone really in control of this?

No, it is impossible for us to control what other people post, tweet and share online. Impossible.

But do we have to believe everything we see?

The answer is no. You have the power to make decisions on what you choose to believe and more importantly how it affects you. This is how you take charge and become in control of social media.

So, let's find out how.

to social media

Social media is an enormous, worldwide platform and there are actually different types of it. Social media includes a range of websites and apps that you may use or know someone who does. They include:

- Social networking sites – Facebook
- Micro blogging sites – Twitter
- Photo sharing sites and apps – Instagram, Snapchat, Pinterest
- Video sharing sites and apps – YouTube, Facebook Live, Vimeo

There are many reasons why people choose to use social media. It may be for personal reasons or for business reasons. Whatever the reason, there are huge advantages in the marvel of social media. Let's explore some of the positive aspects of social media.

Express yourself!

A huge advantage of social media is the platform it gives you to express yourself. You can use your social media page to express your likes and dislikes, share your feelings and mental worries (a great way to relieve yourself of daily stresses!). You can share pictures of what you have been up to. You can join groups and fan pages that reflect your individual personality. These are all fun and enjoyable ways to use social media and are some of the many things it was designed for!

Being able to express yourself online can be valuable to all. People can use social media as an outlet – a way to make their voice heard when they might not have opportunities to do so. To allow those who feel disconnected from the world to connect. To allow those who are struggling to share their worries to seek help. It gives you a space to be you, something we all need.

We are naturally social creatures and it can be rewarding to receive positive comments and likes on the things we share.

Making connections

An incredible benefit of social media is how easy it makes it to keep in touch with family and friends (especially if they live far away!). It offers instant ways of contacting people and keeping up to date with their life – from their likes and dislikes to their relationship status!

Instant messaging means communication is easy! We can make immediate plans with friends and speak to them when we need them; with social media friends are always on hand!

Opportunities

Another advantage to social media, which you may not have come across yet but are likely to in the future, is the opportunities with careers.

Businesses and employers often use social media to share information about potential job opportunities they have – this makes job hunting in the modern day a much easier task that is accessible to all!

Businesses may also use social media to extend their reach to potential customers. Using social media to post and share about a business can lead to more interest from customers and success in profits!

Social media can also be a great tool in helping with your studies. You can create group chats with your friends as study groups to help with difficult school work.

Trending!

Keeping up to date is possible thanks to social media! Social media allows for real-time news discovery, meaning you can access information as soon as it becomes known. News sites will instantly update their social media pages the minute a new story comes in – long gone are the days of waiting for the news to come on in the evening or picking up a fresh newspaper in the morning. Today it is possible for us to keep up with what is trending, meaning never feeling left behind with the latest news or gossip! Being able to keep up with current affairs allow us to make informed decisions about what we know of the world.

Fun fact - 2.77 billion of us use one or more form of social media every single day!

to social media

It is clear why so many of us use social media – there are so many benefits to it! It can boost our self-esteem, allow us to make and keep connections with people, improve our chances of job success and keep us up to date with the world as it is happening.

But… as with lots of things, there are some negative aspects to social media. It is important we recognise these to allow us the knowledge to use social media in the best way possible and most importantly to be in control of it. So, let's explore some of the negatives of social media.

Information overload!

With so many people on social media constantly sharing selfies or tweeting links or posting videos it can become a pretty noisy place. Feeling overwhelmed by too many friends to keep up with online is not uncommon. Over time we come to collect a lot of friends on social media and it can lead to jam-packed news feeds that really we aren't always all that interested in!

 **Have a spring clean – Review your friends list and decide if who you are following makes you feel positive, if not remove them.**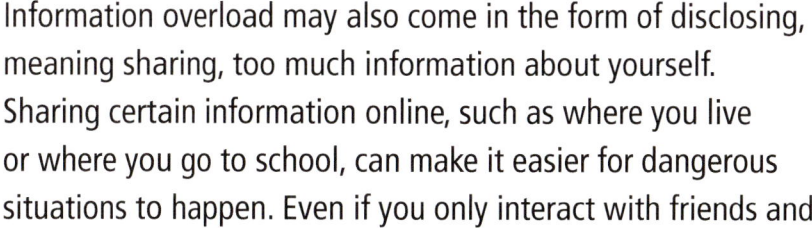

Information overload may also come in the form of disclosing, meaning sharing, too much information about yourself. Sharing certain information online, such as where you live or where you go to school, can make it easier for dangerous situations to happen. Even if you only interact with friends and family online it can be possible for others to access information about you – so remember to check your privacy settings and think about who can see your posts. Consider changing your account settings so it can only be seen by people you accept if you haven't already done so.

Take a second – Before posting or sharing something online take a second to think about the information it is telling others about you. Ask yourself am I sharing too much personal information?

Remember – be safe online, only add and accept people that you know.

Cyber bullying

Cyber bullying, using electronic communication to bully someone, is a huge negative aspect of social media. Today social media means that bullying does not only occur at school but now continues for some people when they get home. Cyber bullying involves sending, posting or sharing content that is harmful, false or mean about another person. It also includes the sharing of private information about someone else with others.

Food for thought – Before posting, sharing or sending a message online ask yourself; would it offend anyone? Am I considering the feelings of others? Am I sharing private information about someone?

Under pressure!

With social media comes social pressures. Struggling to fit in is something many of us have felt and now social media is adding more pressure to that. Being able to see what your peers are doing constantly can add to stresses experienced around not fitting in. Experiencing pressure to keep up with peers is natural but having to interact with it on a regular basis through social media can become overwhelming.

> **Take a break – If browsing on social media is not making you feel good about yourself perhaps it is time to take a break. This may be for a few hours, for a day or for a week, however long you feel you need. It is ok to take a break from social media – you can return to it whenever you like after all! It may be helpful to delete the app from your phone. Use the time you would spend on social media to do something you enjoy – listen to music, go for a walk, or read that book you have been meaning to finish!**

Distraction and procrastination

How often do you see someone looking at their phone? A lot, right? Social media distracts people all the time! Finding reasons to check your social media may in fact be a distraction method to avoid doing what you really should be doing (e.g. homework!). Browsing social media feeds your procrastination habits, your ability to put off doing something (we have all been guilty of this!). You may find talking to your friend or watching videos on social media is making you less productive which may be affecting your school work.

> **Limit the time – If you think social media is causing you to procrastinate or is giving you a reason to be distracted perhaps it is time to limit the time! Set yourself moments in the day when you will allow yourself to go on social media and give them time schedules. This means you can plan your day to get done what you need to and as a result feel better about yourself!**

Social skills?

Despite thinking that social media is social (hence the name!) it can in fact destroy some social skills. Spending a lot of time interacting online can limit social skills you only gain from face to face interactions. You may know someone who is very outspoken on social media but who is actually reserved when it comes to talking face to face. Knowing where to hold your hands or what kind of facial expressions to use is only something to be learnt from interacting in person with others!

> **Arrange a catch up – If you are in need of some face-to-face interaction then arrange a catch up with a friend! Perhaps what you would spend hours messaging your friend about online you could do over a coffee together instead.**

Lifestyle

Using social media involves a lot of sitting down. So spending too much time on it decreases the amount of exercise we are getting. It can also impact on our sleep as the artificial light from a phone or computer screen can affect our ability to get to sleep at night.

Have a cut off – Having a cut off time from social media every day will allow you time to switch off and get a good night's sleep! Set yourself a time in the evening when you can last check your social media, try to make it a couple hours before you normally go to bed.

Fake news

Fake news is a key pitfall of social media. We know social media is positive in keeping us up to date with what is happening, but today there are becoming more and more news stories reported on social media that are not true. This is impacting on people's judgement of the world and their ability to make informed decisions about how news affects them. Sharing fake news stories is also impacting on people's self-esteem and their trust in the media.

Take control – In order to prevent the spreading of fake news it is important that you take responsibility over what you read and share online. Read on to find out more about fake news and how you can take control.

Fake news
R U in control of it?

News. It's everywhere; it's what we know. We listen to it, we see it, we read it and we share it.

But are you in **control of it**? Do you know what news is true? Do you know what news is fake?

Do you feel in **control** of this?

Is anyone in **control** of this?

No, it is impossible for us to control what people tell us, what is published in the newspapers and what is written and shared online. Impossible.

But do we always have to believe everything we are told, read or share?

The answer is no. You have the power to make the choice about what you believe based on what people tell you, what you read and what you see and what you share online. And quite simply, this is how you take charge and become in control of fake news.

So let's find out how we can do this.

First, it is important to know that fake news is not just something you find on social media. The term 'fake news' is directly linked to social media itself but 'false news' can in fact can be shared by newspapers, TV or radio news broadcasting and even when interacting with others. Let's learn more about how false news is shared, so we can take control of it.

We interact with other people all the time and naturally news is shared this way. People often share with each other news they have heard – maybe something to do with them or someone they know or something that is happening in the world. At times people may share news that is false (most of the time without them even knowing!). But do you always believe what you are told? It is fair to say yes when it is coming from someone you trust, but what about when you just aren't sure? How do you know what to believe and what you shouldn't?

It may seem that making decisions about what we believe is pretty simple, we just do it. Our brain decides if someone is telling us something that is true or complete nonsense, right?

Actually … our brain is working a lot harder to make that decision than you may think. It is using more knowledge than you may realise.

The words are not enough!

It is rare for our brains to just listen to words being said and decide whether to believe them. In fact, when we are listening to another person our brain is looking at a much wider picture than just the words coming out.

People do not just use words to communicate: they also use their body language. Body language is itself a form of language; it is the physical movements we use to communicate information. The interesting thing about body language is we do not always know we are using it. It is a mix of conscious, meaning aware, and unconscious, meaning unaware, movements that we express to show our attitudes and feelings towards what we are saying to another person. These physical movements can include facial expressions, body posture, gestures, eye movements and the use of the space around you.

Body posture – the way someone positions their body when they are talking to you can often show their emotions towards what they are saying.

Gestures – the movements someone makes with their body parts (usually their hands, arms and head) can communicate to you how relaxed and comfortable they are about what they are saying.

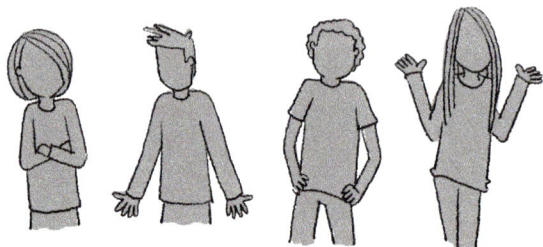

Eye movements – the movements made by someone's eyes can communicate different meanings about what they are saying. Eye movements can express someone's interest and self-belief in what they are communicating. Interestingly, eye movements have different meanings in different cultures.

Space – how someone uses the space around them when communicating can also express their emotions and comfort in what they are saying. Again, the meaning of use of space differs in cultures.

Although meanings do differ amongst cultures, what they do have in common is their use by humans around the world to express their emotions behind what they are saying.

So, body language is the nonverbal or physical signals you use to communicate, whilst words are the verbal signals. Our brain independently takes in more information from the nonverbal signals used by another person and they massively influence the decision-making part of the brain.

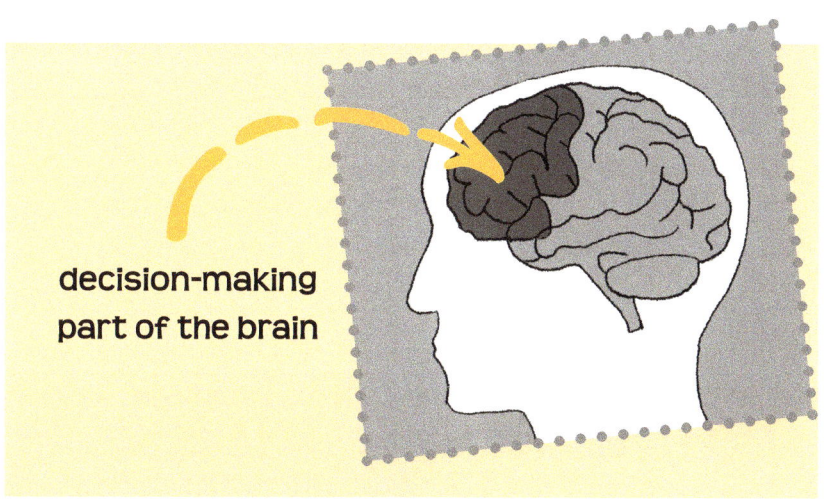

decision-making part of the brain

Body language in action

Body language is such a powerful tool of communication that being an expert in reading body language proves extremely useful in a range of jobs.

- ⭐ Detectives and criminal investigators use body language clues to make decisions about the information given by suspects or witnesses of crimes.

- ⭐ Speech and language therapists use body language to help them understand what patients are trying to communicate.

- ⭐ Interpreters, although fluent in languages, may use body language to improve the accuracy of their translation.

- ⭐ Reading body language proves useful when playing the game poker. Players use it to spot their opponents cheating or to work out when they are doing well.

If someone is telling you something, and you are unsure if you should believe them, ask yourself these questions:

- ✘ What is the person's body language showing me? Does it show the right emotions to match what they are saying?

- ✘ How are they using their body posture and gestures to communicate? Do they seem comfortable about what they are saying?

 **Remember – body language and its meaning varies in different cultures. Consider how your culture uses body language.**

SUMMARY

Whilst your ears are listening to the words you are being told, your brain is observing the body language to support your decision-making abilities. It helps you to make choices about what you believe based on what others are saying, meaning we don't have to rely on words alone. It is a powerful tool we use to take control.

But what about when words are all we have? What about when it is not someone telling us, but something? What about the things we read or hear?

Newspapers, television and radio broadcasting are all forms of news in the media – so how do we know if what we are reading or hearing there is true? How can we take control over false news in the media? Let's find out more.

Newspapers – A source of everyday information read by on average 2.5 billion people across the world every day. Newspapers contain information about current events and have been circulating as early as 1566. Many consider newspapers to be a credible source of information, meaning they can be trusted.

Magazines – A source of information based on a particular subject of interest to the reader. Magazine subjects differ massively from cars to wildlife or from golf to knitting. It is a huge and wide-ranging media source. Some magazines are also a source of news – this may be political news, world news or celebrity news.

Newspapers and magazines are both easy ways to access news, and every single day they tell billions of people what to believe. But should they believe? Are they a source of accurate information? It is hard to say. Some are considered more credible than others as over time they have built a national reputation in being reliable (meaning consistently true). But some have not. Some are believed to publish stories that are **not completely accurate**, all because of an agenda.

Agenda – This is a word you might hear when discussing if newspapers or magazines publish factual stories. So, what is an agenda? Having an agenda means to have a hidden purpose or intention behind what you are doing or what you are saying – that the other person may not know about. It may mean that you tell someone something that is not accurate, just so they believe you.

This can be innocent. You may tell your friend that the cupcakes they baked were delicious even though really you did not like them. All because you think you are telling them what they want to hear, right? A nice thing to do, after all we all like to make people happy.

But when it comes to the media and newspapers especially, it can have bigger consequences. Naturally, people rely on newspapers to inform their understanding of the world they live in. If newspapers are publishing stories that are not accurate then it could falsely impact a person's views and opinions, allowing them to be skewed by information that is not completely true.

Here are a couple of examples of false news stories that have been reported by newspapers and magazines in the past.

- ✘ The Great Moon Hoax – 1835 – A series of articles were published in the New York Sun claiming that life on the Moon had been discovered. After gaining lots of new subscribers (as a result of the false news drawing people in!), the paper admitted the articles were false.

- ✘ The Cottingley Fairies – 1917 – Elsie Wright and Frances Griffiths took several photographs in their garden which they claimed to be of fairies. The photographs were used in a magazine article claiming the existence of fairies. It turned out the two girls had cut pictures of fairies out of a book and attached them to trees using hatpins. It was not until 1980 that they admitted the photographs were faked.

It might be fair to think of these articles as funny or a harmless joke, but they actually have a bigger effect on the reader than you may at first think. Innocently, believing a false news story may feel embarrassing, but more dangerously it can it impact your judgement of the world and negatively affect your views and opinions. Reporting false news stories is damaging people's trust in the media and their self-esteem.

SUMMARY

Newspapers and magazines can be accurate sources of information, but they often alter information to meet an agenda. They may exaggerate or change the detail of a news story to meet a message they want to send out for people to believe, to suit what they want people to act upon. This may sound scary and might make you want to never pick up a newspaper, but that does not have to be the case. We can all read newspapers and magazines to engage with what is happening around the world but we can make our own decisions about what we choose to believe. This is you taking control over what you read.

Hearing about the news

The news we hear on the television or on the radio is known as news broadcasting. This type of news can be produced locally – sharing events about a local area or by a broadcast network – sharing events from around the world. Both may also report information on sports, weather forecasts, traffic reports and any other material that the broadcaster feels is relevant to their audience.

Broadcasters will present news stories in a manner that will successfully reach their audience – meaning at times detail may be slightly altered or exaggerated to get their attention, resulting in some level of false news.

It is fair to consider broadcasting media a trustworthy source of news. As television news will likely include video footage of the event and similarly radio news will use sound bites of the event – showing an actual news story as it occurred. By doing so we are seeing or hearing an accurate report of the news, which we can make our own judgement of.

However where false news comes into play with news broadcasting is in its ability to constantly change. As this type of news is often reported as the story is happening it naturally means it is often changing – giving you mixed messages. They may start off by telling you one thing but the next hour this fact has completely or slightly changed. This is because the story itself has changed or because the view of the broadcasting company has. Either way it may be valuable to bear this in mind when hearing about the news.

SUMMARY

News reported on the television or radio is known as news broadcasting. This news is often more factual as it uses video clips and sound bites of actual news stories. News broadcasting often reports in real-time meaning the stories or views of the broadcasting company are often changing. This can naturally lead to the reporting of false news.

So, let's take control over what we read and hear!

There is one main thing we need to know to take control over false news in the media – knowledge of how it is gathered and presented. From this we can decide how factual and accurate a story is.

So how is printed news created?

Stage 1 – News reporters gather stories and cover events. They talk to the public, the people of interest or the witnesses of big events that have just occurred. Reporters work hard to collect and gather the information they need to create a story suitable for their newspaper or magazine. This story will be edited and finalised.

Stage 2 – Once finalised, editors, with their agendas in mind, will gather to determine which of the finalised stories will go in that day. Each page will be planned, and the graphics will be added. It will be ready for print.

Stage 3 – The printing process requires quickness and reliability. Printers can print multiple pages at once and at high quality. Machines then sort and fold the pages.

Stage 4 – Copies are then collected and transported off for selling.

How is broadcast news created?

Stage 1 – Broadcast news is collected in a similar way to printed news with reporters gathering stories and events by interviewing people of interest or witnesses.

Stage 2 – News broadcasting also involves an editor who has overall control and the final say on which stories will be covered, for how long and in what order. They will decide on how the story is presented on the television or radio. The editor is responsible for the accuracy and style of the programme.

Stage 3 – The reporter will then create a 'package' (the edited news piece created for the programme) for the presenter in the television or radio studio to read.

Now, did you identify where false news could have occurred in the processes? Where were decisions made on what news stories to report based on the decision of the editor? In stage 2. It was here that the editors chose the stories based on what they want to share, what they want people to know and what they want people to believe.

Being wise, taking control!

So, by knowing this we can now question – why has the story been chosen and how is it being presented? Questioning this allows us to take control over the impact we let news have on us.

When doing so consider these questions:
- What is the purpose of this story?
- What is this story trying to tell me? (Think agenda!)

Then ask yourself:
- Does the content of this story match that of other media coverage?

- Are the facts and figures of this story the same as the ones being reported by other media sources?
- Does it support what I believe?
- Does it represent reality?

If it does then perhaps it is factual and you can take control in believing it, which is ok. If it does not, then maybe it is somewhat false and you can take control in choosing not to be influenced by it and that too is ok. Whatever the outcome remember you have taken control, and you have made your own decision about how it impacts you.

To note – we may at times come across situations when we are confused about whether we believe something in the media. Perhaps the purpose keeps changing or the facts and figures do. That is ok; you may find it useful to discuss it with an adult you trust. This may be your parents, a family member or your teachers. Speaking to them may help you find out more about the story. This could help you to make a better decision.

SUMMARY

The media is an important and easy way to access news. It allows us to keep up to date with current issues, helping us to make informed decisions about our life. But some sources are more trusted than others. Remember that some have agendas, so take control by asking yourself questions or seeking advice from an adult you trust about how news in the media should impact you.

Ok, so we know how to take control over the news we experience in the media.

But (there's always a but!)… as we know, today there is a huge area where news is shared on an instant and constant basis; social media. And with 2.77 billion of us on social media it is easy to understand how fake news is shared so easily.

Rise of fake news!

By now you feel in control of the news you are told, the news you read and the news you see and hear. But are you in control of the news you see and share online?

Taking control over what you share on social media is a must thanks to the rise of fake news. So, what exactly is online fake news?

Fake news is a term that did not even exist a few years ago but now is something you hear a lot. As we know, fake news basically means news stories shared on the Internet that are not true. These stories may **not be completely accurate** or may be **completely false**; either way they are examples of fake news.

Some stories will have some truth to them, but are not completely accurate. This will be because the person who wrote the story (perhaps a journalist or an online blogger) did not check all the facts before they published the story. Or they may have exaggerated some of it to relate to their online followers.

Other stories will be completely false, meaning they have no truth to them whatsoever. The person who wrote the story will know it is made up and these stories have been intentionally published online and shared around to make people believe something that is not true.

Fun fact – The term 'fake news' is so huge that it was named 2017's word of the year!

Fake news is a problem, like any other false news, as it causes people to believe things that are not true. It can change their beliefs, views and opinions based on deliberate lies and impact their judgements of the world. Fake news is also leading to a rise in people having less trust in social media.

So why are we talking about fake news so much?

As we know fake news is a new wonder, the term has only just come into existence. We know the telling of half-truths has existed as long as humans have communicated, and the concept of publishing not completely accurate news has been around for a long time (as we know with newspaper agendas!). But the idea of publishing **completely false** information is a new and modern danger.

Did you know?

The term fake news entered our vocabulary thanks to the 2016 USA election, when Donald Trump was elected president. He put down a reporter who questioned him about a news article published online, with the now famous phrase "You are fake news!" During the presidential election there was a huge increase in the evidence of fake news – a large number of fake stories were published about Donald Trump and his opponent Hillary Clinton. The danger came, as these fake news stories were believed to have impacted on how people chose to vote (despite the information being completely or partially false!). This shows just how persuasive fake news is and how it impacts and misleads a person's view on the world.

Have a look at some of these fake news stories.

Again, it is fair to think of some of these articles as funny. They may also seem like a harmless joke, but they too are having a bigger effect on the reader. When we read news articles online that are of interest to us or to someone we know we may share the article, meaning we will post it on our own social media page for our followers/friends to see. You may have done this yourself, only to later find that the article is false or not completely true.

This is understandably making people feel quite silly. You may feel embarrassed that you believed the article in the first place or that you passed on information to others that is not true. It can damage our self-esteem, as we may feel uncertain about our own beliefs or what we thought we knew. It is reducing further our trust in media and even the government systems that represent our country.

It is not a nice feeling, but it is ok. Many of us have been there! Although to avoid it again, let's take control over fake news!

So, let's take control over fake news!

To take control over fake news we need to know how it is made and more importantly why. This will give us the knowledge to tackle fake news and the confidence to continue sharing news articles online that we know are true!

Why do people create fake news?

Let's explore some of the reasons why fake news is created:

Political reasons
Fake news is created mostly for political reasons. Writers of fake news stories often want to push a political agenda (there's that word again!), meaning they want people to believe something for a political gain such as votes in an election. This type of fake news is also called propaganda.

Entertainment reasons
Some fake news is created for entertainment. The stories will have a huge amount of exaggeration and are often about celebrities.

Financial reasons
Money is a big reason why fake news exists. Fake news stories are often published on websites then shared on social media to increase the number of visitors to that site. The writers will come up with exciting headlines to grab the reader's attention so they are more likely to click on the story to read it. The more clicks to the website, the more money is made. This money comes from advertising. Stories therefore have to be really exciting so writers will exaggerate or invent them. Creating fake news for money is also known as **Clickbait**.

Ok so we know reasons why fake news is created, we know it exists and we know it is a problem. So, just how can we tackle it? How can we take control over fake news?

Being wise, taking control

It is important that we can identify fake news online then we can read and share news correctly and confidently. So when reading a news article online ask yourself these questions to find out how fake it really is:

- Firstly, is the story believable? Is it realistic to what you know of the world?
- Have you heard of the website it is published on?
- Does the website look professional?
- Do the photos/videos in the article look normal?
- Does the website address look normal? (Is the end something like **.org**, **.co.uk** or **.com** not something like **.com.co**?)
- Do other websites report the same facts? (Have a quick Google!)
- Has the story also been reported on the TV, radio or in a trustworthy newspaper? (If the same story has been published in a variety of places with the **SAME** facts then it is likely to be true!)

If you feel the answer to all, some, or even one of these questions is no then it may be worth spending a bit more time researching the facts before sharing the story with others.

 **Remember – if you are still unsure talk to an adult you trust (parent, family member or teacher) about the story to find out more about it.**

Knowing what's real and what's fake online can help you to take control, to think for yourself and to be confident in what you are sharing. You will gain a better understanding of the world and trust in the media.

You're not alone in the fight!

Fake news is such a huge problem that is reassuring to know social media sites are now working to tackle it themselves. Sites are working hard to close down accounts that share fake news and to keep political stories and advertisements to a minimum. Many social media users are taking control after being encouraged to report false information online.

SUMMARY

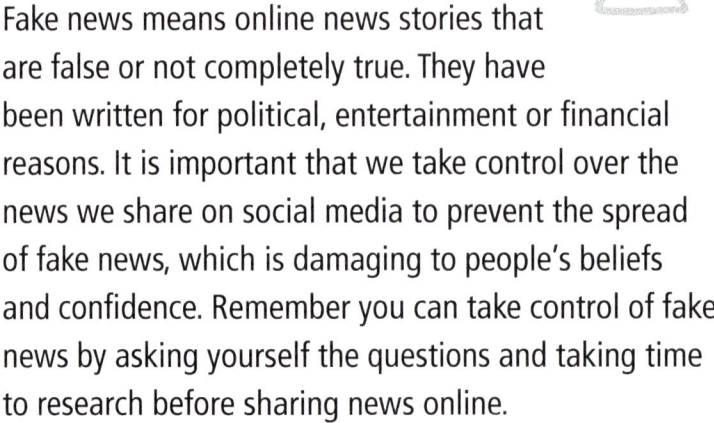

Fake news means online news stories that are false or not completely true. They have been written for political, entertainment or financial reasons. It is important that we take control over the news we share on social media to prevent the spread of fake news, which is damaging to people's beliefs and confidence. Remember you can take control of fake news by asking yourself the questions and taking time to research before sharing news online.

Ok, so we have learnt a lot about taking control. We know we can take control over fake news. We know we can take control over the news people tell us, the news we read and the news we share online.

We are well equipped with questions to use as tips and tricks to take control. Here they are summarised below, read them and then re-read them. Be wise, take control:

When talking about news ask yourself –

- What is the person's body language showing me? Does it reflect the right emotions based on what they are saying?
- How are they using their body posture and gestures to communicate? Do they appear comfortable about what they are saying?

When engaging with news in the media ask yourself –

- What was the purpose of this story?
- What is this story trying to tell me? (Think agenda!)
- Does the content of this story match that of other media coverage?
- Are the facts and figures of this story the same as the ones being reported on other media coverage?
- Does that support what I believe?
- Does it represent reality?

And if in doubt – find out more information from an adult you trust.

And, when reading and sharing news online ask yourself:

- Firstly, is the story believable? Is it realistic to what you know of the world?
- Have you heard of the website it is published on?
- Does the website look professional?
- Do the photos/videos in the article look normal?
- Does the website address look normal? (Is the end something like **.org**, **.co.uk** or **.com** not something like **.com.co**?)
- Do other websites report the same facts? (Have a quick Google!)
- Has the story also been reported on the TV, radio or a trustworthy newspaper?

Quiz time!

Now you're equipped with the knowledge to tackle fake news, have a go at this quiz (keep practising until you get them all!).

1. Other than words, what does our brain assess to make decisions about what we believe when communicating with others?
2. Can you name two types of it?
3. What word might you may hear when discussing if newspapers or magazines write the truth?
4. What is the term given to news that is reported on the television or radio?

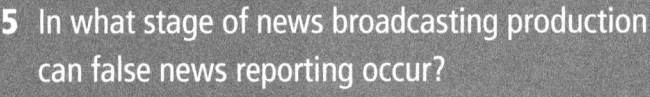

5. In what stage of news broadcasting production can false news reporting occur?
6. Where will you mostly find fake news?
7. Is fake news stories that are completely false, not completely true, or both?
8. Can you name a reason why fake news is created?
9. Can you name at least two questions you should ask yourself before sharing news online?

Find the answers on the last page. Did you get them all? Well done; you can spot fake news! You are in control!

1. You are in control – you have the choice and the ability to take control over what you believe and how news impacts you.

2. Take comfort in knowing your brain is a powerful tool in taking control and is working hard without us knowing to do so!

3. Don't be afraid to read newspapers or magazines – just remember they have agendas and can sometimes exaggerate a story. Speak to an adult you trust to learn more about printed media and their agendas to make better sense of them and which ones may suit you to read.

4. Have trust in news broadcasting, on the television or the radio – just remember that it can constantly change so take time to consider how it is influencing you.

5. Don't be afraid of news online – just treat it wisely! Remember that fake news exists and is available on social media. Ensure you research a story before sharing it online – this will improve your confidence on social media.

6. Have confidence in yourself knowing you have learnt to take control. Share what you have learnt with friends and family!

Quiz answers

1 Body language

2 Body posture, gestures, eye movements, space

3 Agenda

4 News broadcasting

5 Stage 2

6 Online through social media

7 Both

8 Political, entertainment or financial (money)

9 Any 2 questions from page 45

Written by Aimée Jackson
Edited by Josephine Herrlinger
Illustrated by Charlie Alder
Designed by Sarah Peden Aspinall

Copyright © 2019 BrambleKids Ltd.
All rights reserved.

ISBN 978-1-911625-70-4